INSIDE MLS

HOUSTON DYNAMO

BY ANTHONY K. HEWSON

abdobooks.com

Published by Abdo Publishing, a division of ABDO, PO Box 398166, Minneapolis, Minnesota 55439. Copyright © 2022 by Abdo Consulting Group, Inc. International copyrights reserved in all countries. No part of this book may be reproduced in any form without written permission from the publisher. SportsZone™ is a trademark and logo of Abdo Publishing.

Printed in the United States of America, North Mankato, Minnesota
052021
092021

THIS BOOK CONTAINS RECYCLED MATERIALS

Cover Photo: Melissa Phillip/Houston Chronicle/AP Images
Interior Photos: Kevin Buehler/Odessa American/AP Images, 5, 6; Matt Slocum/AP Images, 9, 11, 13, 34; Focus on Sport/Getty Images Sport/Getty Images, 15; Pat Sullivan/AP Images, 17; James Nielsen/Houston Chronicle/AP Images, 19; Haraz Ghanbari/AP Images, 20, 37; David J. Phillip/AP Images, 23, 43; Bob Levey/AP Images, 25, 27, 28; Trask Smith/Cal Sport Media/AP Images, 31; Andrew Richardson/Cal Sport Media/AP Images, 33; Pablo Martinez Monsivais/AP Images, 39; Leslie Plaza Johnson/Icon Sportswire/AP Images, 40

Editor: Patrick Donnelly
Series Designer: Dan Peluso

Library of Congress Control Number: 2019954321

Publisher's Cataloging-in-Publication Data
Names: Hewson, Anthony K., author.
Title: Houston Dynamo / by Anthony K. Hewson
Description: Minneapolis, Minnesota : Abdo Publishing, 2022 | Series: Inside MLS | Includes online resources and index.
Identifiers: ISBN 9781532192579 (lib. bdg.) | ISBN 9781644945650 (pbk.) | ISBN 9781098210472 (ebook)
Subjects: LCSH: Houston Dynamo (Soccer team)--Juvenile literature. | Soccer teams--Juvenile literature. | Professional sports franchises--Juvenile literature. | Sports Teams--Juvenile literature.
Classification: DDC 796.334--dc23

TABLE OF CONTENTS

CHAPTER 1
WELCOME TO HOUSTON 4

CHAPTER 2
A SHAKEUP IN MLS 14

CHAPTER 3
HOUSTON'S HEROES 24

CHAPTER 4
DYNAMITE MOMENTS 34

TIMELINE	44
TEAM FACTS	45
GLOSSARY	46
MORE INFORMATION	47
ONLINE RESOURCES	47
INDEX	48
ABOUT THE AUTHOR	48

CHAPTER 1

WELCOME TO HOUSTON

A wave of orange flowed up Interstate 45 in east-central Texas on November 12, 2006. It was a four-hour drive from Houston to Frisco, Texas, the location of Pizza Hut Park. But it was a trip Houston Dynamo fans were happy to make. That's because when they arrived, they would watch their team play for the Major League Soccer (MLS) Cup.

A local business owner helped organize a caravan of buses to bring fans to the match. Hundreds more fans took their own cars, many of which were decorated in the Dynamo colors of orange and white. The dedication was impressive considering that just one year earlier, the Dynamo didn't even exist.

Fans of the Houston Dynamo packed the stands to cheer on their club in the 2006 MLS Cup.

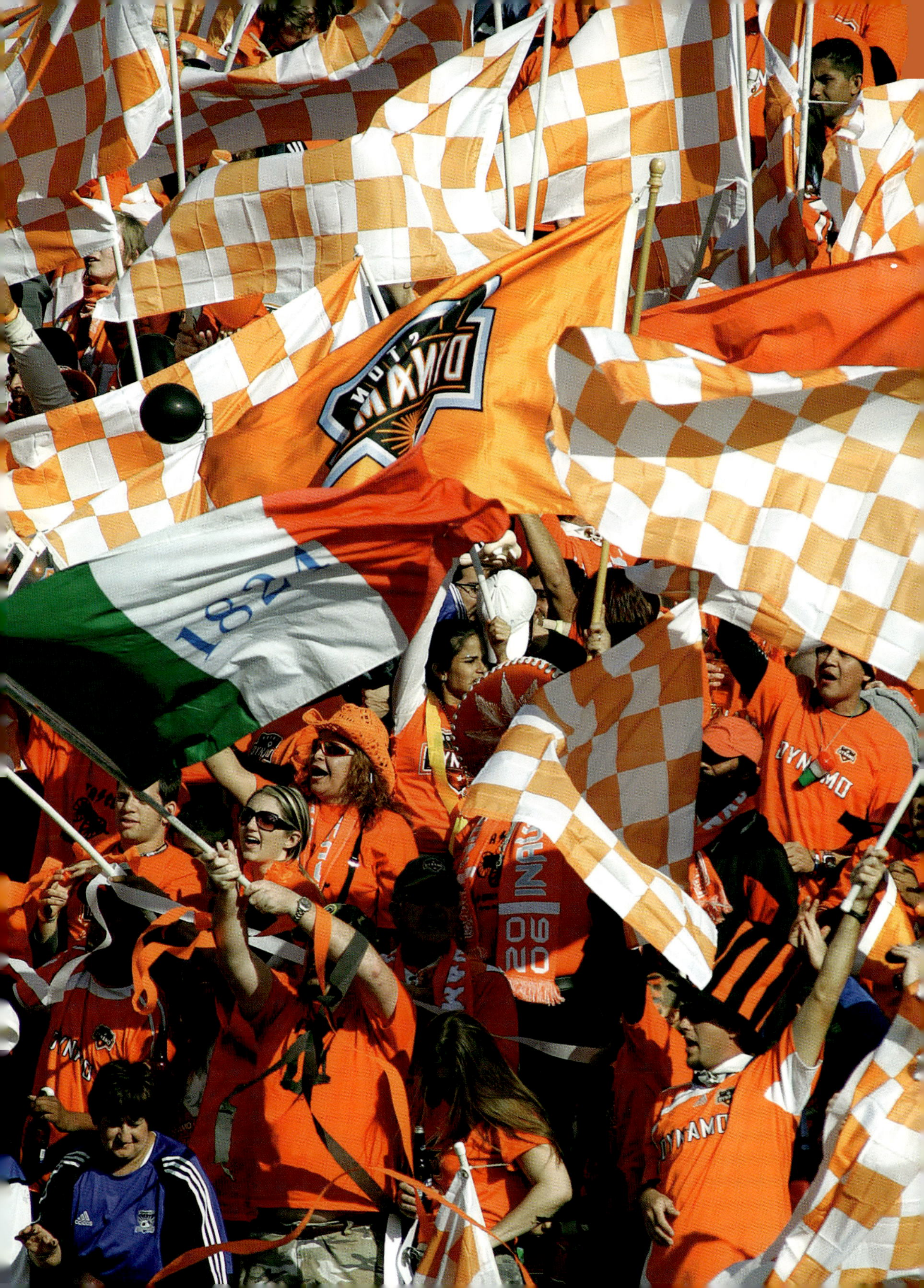
1824
DYNAMO
DYNAMO

Revolution midfielder Joe Franchino (8) tries to hold off Houston's Brian Mullan as they fight for a loose ball.

    The previous December, MLS Commissioner Don Garber announced the San Jose Earthquakes were moving. They would leave behind that name and history in California while starting over in Houston. The team was already primed for a championship run. The Earthquakes were a regular playoff team that had won the MLS Cup in 2001 and 2003.

DUEL AT FORWARD

Brian Ching was one of the stars moving to Houston with the team. He was also a forward on the US national team. Ching led the Dynamo in scoring in 2006 and was a big reason why they were in the final.

Across the field in the MLS Cup was Ching's US teammate, New England Revolution forward Taylor Twellman. The two were friends but had a competitive rivalry. Twellman had been left off the American roster for that year's World Cup. Ching made the team but did not get off the bench during the tournament. Both strikers believed they had something to prove, and they played big roles in the MLS Cup.

One of the game's first scoring chances was Twellman's. In the 25th minute, the Revolution built up a play through midfield. New England's Joe Franchino sent in a crossing pass toward the goal. Twellman was there for a header. But he did not make good contact, lightly sending the ball towards the net where it was easily saved. Twellman grabbed his head in frustration.

ROUTE TO THE FINAL

Houston's championship run almost ended in the first round. The Dynamo suffered a 2–1 loss in the first of a two-match semifinal round against Chivas USA. But they rebounded in the second match to win 2–0 and advance by aggregate. Ching scored in the 93rd minute to clinch the victory. The Dynamo then handled the Colorado Rapids at home 3–1 to advance to the MLS Cup.

The Revolution tried to add to their scoring attack. It helped they had another US national team star on the bench in Clint Dempsey. He did not start due to an ankle injury. The Revs brought him on as a substitute in the second half. But neither he nor anyone else on New England could beat the Houston defense.

New England's defense did its job too. Because of this, scoring chances were rare. The Revolution had one of the game's best opportunities in the 86th minute. Jay Heaps headed the ball towards goal for his teammate Twellman. But Ching arrived to clear the ball away in the nick of time, just before Twellman could get to it.

The match headed to extra time tied at 0–0. Finally, in the 113th minute, Twellman was able to bag a goal. He fired a shot that just rolled past the outstretched arm of Dynamo keeper Pat Onstad. New England just had to hang on for seven minutes to win its first championship.

Dynamo goalkeeper Pat Onstad, *right*, prevents Revolution forward Clint Dempsey from scoring during overtime of the MLS Cup.

But the lead didn't even last a minute. Shortly after the kickoff to restart the game, Ching made a run toward the goal. Teammate Brian Mullan lofted in a crossing pass. Ching leaped and got his head to it. The ball shot past New England goalkeeper Matt Reis. Just like that, the score was tied again.

DOWN TO A SHOOTOUT

Neither team could score in the rest of extra time. So for the first time in the 10-year history of the MLS Cup, a championship would be decided by penalty kicks. Each team chose five players for the shootout. For New England, that even included keeper Reis, who converted his chance.

After four rounds, each team had missed once. It was Ching's turn. He started his run and paused slightly, trying to fool Reis. He then struck the ball and buried it to the keeper's left. With one kick left to go, New England had to convert or Houston would be champions.

Heaps stepped up for the Revolution. With the orange-clad fans going crazy, he stared down the ball. He started his run. Heaps tried to place the ball accurately rather than go for power. But the shot was much too weak. It rolled slowly to Onstad, who fell to his right and saved it easily.

Brian Ching celebrates his game-tying goal in overtime.

CHAMPIONS' CUP PLAY

The win in the 2006 MLS Cup earned Houston the right to represent MLS in the 2007 Concacaf Champions' Cup. The tournament, now called the Champions League, featured the best teams from North and Central America and the Caribbean.

The Dynamo made it to the semifinals, where they faced Mexico league champion Pachuca in a two-match series. Houston even won the first match at home 2–0. But Pachuca rallied in the second match in Mexico, exploding for five goals to advance by an aggregate score of 5–4.

The crowd erupted. Onstad sprinted to the sideline and slid on his knees in front of the Houston fans, holding the ball proudly in the air. Onstad's Dynamo teammates sprinted to him and mobbed him in celebration.

Ching was named the game's Most Valuable Player (MVP). He and his teammates then hoisted the MLS Cup trophy and paraded it around the stadium. It had been a wild year for the players. They started over in a new city and earned new fans on their way to a championship.

For the city of Houston, it was its first major professional championship since the Women's National Basketball Association's Comets won in 2000. Houston's sports fans were hungry for more success. They now had a championship soccer team to call their own. And the Dynamo were not done winning just yet.

Dynamo captain Wade Barrett hoists the championship trophy after Houston defeated New England in the 2006 MLS Cup.

CHAPTER 2

A SHAKEUP IN MLS

Professional soccer in Houston did not start with the Dynamo. In fact, the Dynamo team that began play in 2006 was not even the first to use that name. The history of soccer in Space City dates back to the 1960s. The most prominent US pro league prior to MLS was the North American Soccer League (NASL). The NASL lasted from 1968 to 1984.

Two different teams represented Houston in the NASL. The Houston Stars joined in 1968 but folded after the season. Then the Houston Hurricane played from 1978 to 1980. The Hurricane won a division title in 1979, but otherwise, neither team had much success.

Kyle Rote Jr. was one of the stars of the short-lived Houston Hurricane of the NASL.

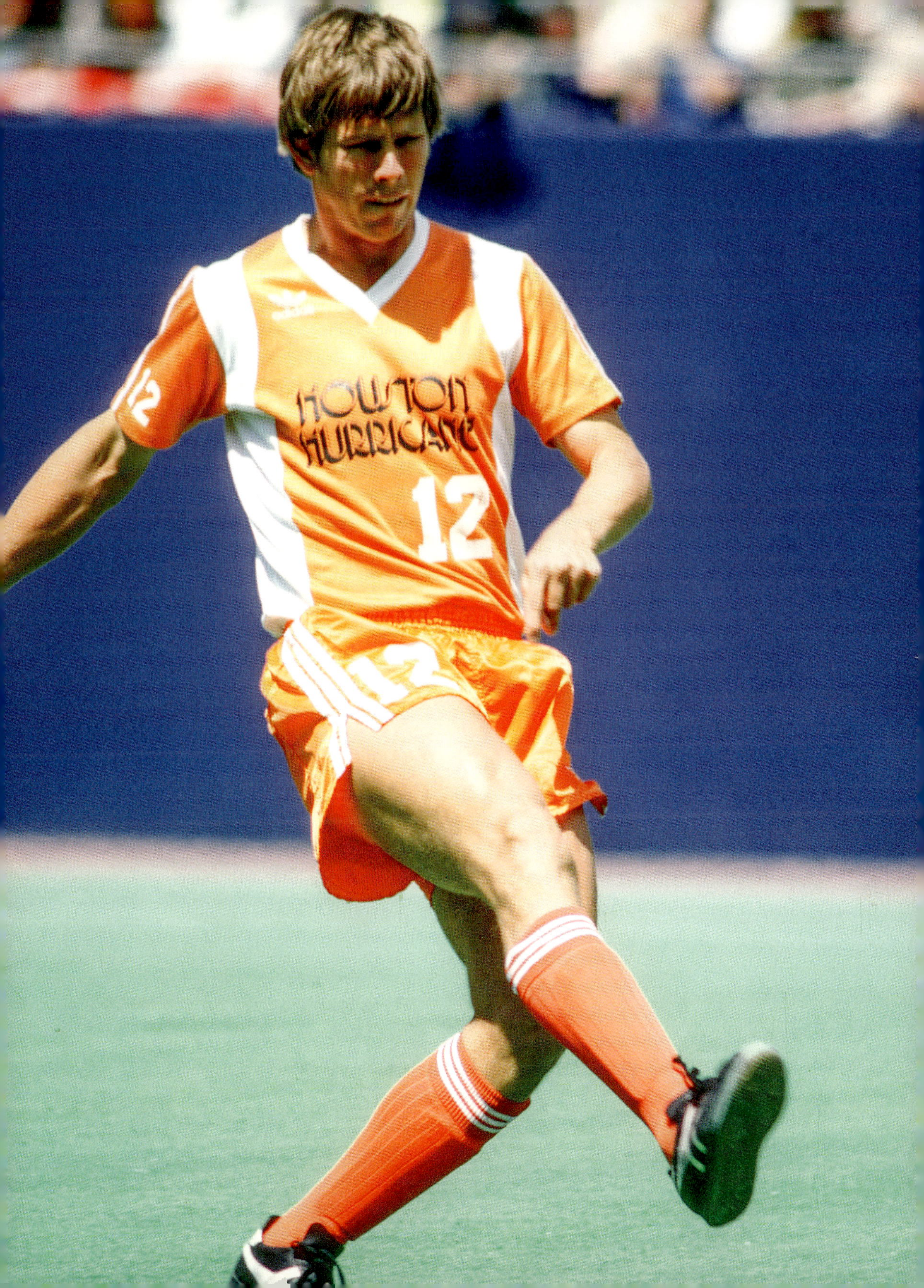
HOUSTON
HURRICANE
12

The longest-lived professional team in Houston soccer was the Houston Dynamos of the United Soccer League (USL). They played from 1984 to 1991, nearly winning the USL championship in their first season. The Houston Summit was a charter franchise of the Major Indoor Soccer League (MISL). But the Summit lasted just two seasons, making the MISL finals in 1980, their last season. Finally, another indoor team called the Houston Hotshots played from 1994 to 2000.

Houston was without a pro team from 2000 to 2005. But the city didn't lose its appetite for soccer. If anything, it had only grown. Houston had a large Hispanic population, and soccer is the most popular sport in many Spanish-speaking countries. Houston regularly hosted Mexico's national team in matches that drew huge crowds.

THE ROAD LEADS TO HOUSTON

MLS considered Houston prime territory to place a team. And in 2005, one team was in need of a home. The San Jose Earthquakes were an original MLS team. They had won two MLS Cups, but their attendance was poor. The team's owners planned to sell the team to a group that could build them a new stadium. But when that sale fell through, the only willing buyers were in Houston.

Team captain Wade Barrett signs autographs in front of the Houston 1836 logo. That team name didn't last long, however.

On December 15, 2005, it was official. The Earthquakes were moving to Houston. But the Earthquakes' name didn't make sense there. And MLS said San Jose would get another team someday. So the Earthquakes' name, colors, and history all remained in California. All of the team employees, including the players and coaches, moved to Houston, but MLS considered the Dynamo a new team.

On January 25, 2006, the team announced its new name: Houston 1836. The colors were orange and white, and the logo featured the club name inside a star. It was a fitting look for the Lone Star State. The name referenced the year Houston was founded and the year Texas gained independence from Mexico.

However, to some members of the city's Mexican population, the name didn't inspire positive feelings. Texas and Mexico were embroiled in war in 1836. Mexico's army was defeated that year at the Battle of San Jacinto during Texas's war for independence.

The team did not want to exclude anybody, as it was aiming to represent all of Houston. In March the team announced it was changing its name to the Dynamo. The new name was not only a reference to the earlier Houston Dynamos. It also represented Houston's thriving oil and gas industry. The name sounded energetic and was also a popular name for soccer teams around the world.

A DYNAMIC START

Less than a month before its first game, the team finally had a name. But would it have any fans? That question was answered quickly. More than 25,000 new Dynamo fans showed up for the team's first home game on April 2, 2006. And they went home happy, as Brian Ching netted four goals in Houston's 5–2 win over the Colorado Rapids.

Houston's Ricardo Clark, *left*, challenges Colorado's Nicolas Hernandez during the Dynamo's first game on April 2, 2006.

The Dynamo made it two in a row when they repeated as MLS Cup champions in 2007.

    The Dynamo played their first six seasons at Robertson Stadium on the University of Houston campus. And Houstonians got to see a lot of winning on that field. Ching was the team's top scorer, but he was assisted on offense by midfielders Dwayne De Rosario, Stu Holden, and Ricardo Clark. Houston repeated as MLS Cup champs in 2007, becoming the second team in league history to win back-to-back titles.

An attempt for an unprecedented three MLS Cups in a row fell short in 2008. In a two-game matchup in the conference semifinals, Houston got off to a good start with a 1–1 draw on the road against the New York Red Bulls. But when the series switched to Houston, New York posted a dominant 3–0 victory to advance. The 2009 team advanced out of the semis but was shut out 2–0 by the LA Galaxy in the conference final.

De Rosario, Holden, and Clark were all gone by 2010, and the team missed the playoffs. A new group of scorers joined Ching for 2011, including Will Bruin and Brad Davis. Houston made back-to-back MLS Cup finals in 2011 and 2012 but lost both times. Both losses came to the Galaxy.

The team entered a new era in 2012 when it opened BBVA Compass Stadium. After playing for six years in a stadium designed for American football, the team would now play in a new downtown stadium built specifically for soccer. It was smaller and got fans closer to the action. Add that to the sometimes-brutal Texas heat, and Houston became a tough place for opponents to play.

Big changes were coming for Houston. Ching retired after 2013, then longtime general manager and coach Dominic Kinnear resigned in 2014. The team missed the MLS playoffs

SUPERSTAR OWNER

The Dynamo added an MVP to the front office in 2019. National Basketball Association star James Harden bought a share of ownership in the Dynamo. Harden played for the Houston Rockets at the time and is also a huge soccer fan.

that season. From 2014 to 2019 the Dynamo reached the playoffs just once. One bright spot came in 2018. With new high-scoring forward Mauro Manotas, Houston won its first US Open Cup title. Winning that tournament, which is open to every men's soccer club in the country, was a sign that Houston might be ready to turn the corner.

After the 2019 season, the Dynamo signed former US men's national team hero Tab Ramos as its next head coach. Ramos was the first player to sign an MLS contract when the league was formed in 1996. He had been coaching the US U-20 men's team. Turning the Dynamo around would be a tough task, though. Ramos got some help when the team acquired a new striker in Darwin Quintero and a new goalkeeper in Marko Marić. Although Houston missed the playoffs for the third season in a row, Quintero tied for the MLS lead in assists, and Marić was second in saves.

Houston's Romell Quioto fights for the ball with two Philadelphia Union players in the 2018 US Open Cup final. Houston won 3–0.

23

CHAPTER 3

HOUSTON'S
HEROES

Brian Ching's Dynamo career may have started in San Jose, but he will always be remembered as a Houstonian. It would be difficult to make a bigger entrance than Ching did in Houston's first-ever game. He scored the first goal in Dynamo history. Then he scored the second, and the third, and the fourth. Ching was just the seventh MLS player ever to score four goals in a game.

Ching kept racking up the goals from there. He scored 69 in his Dynamo career. That was the most in club history when he retired in 2013. Ching was also a key player on the US men's national team. He made 45 international appearances and scored 11 goals. In Ching's final year of playing, he also served as an assistant coach for the Dynamo.

Brian Ching made a habit of scoring big goals during his eight seasons with the Dynamo.

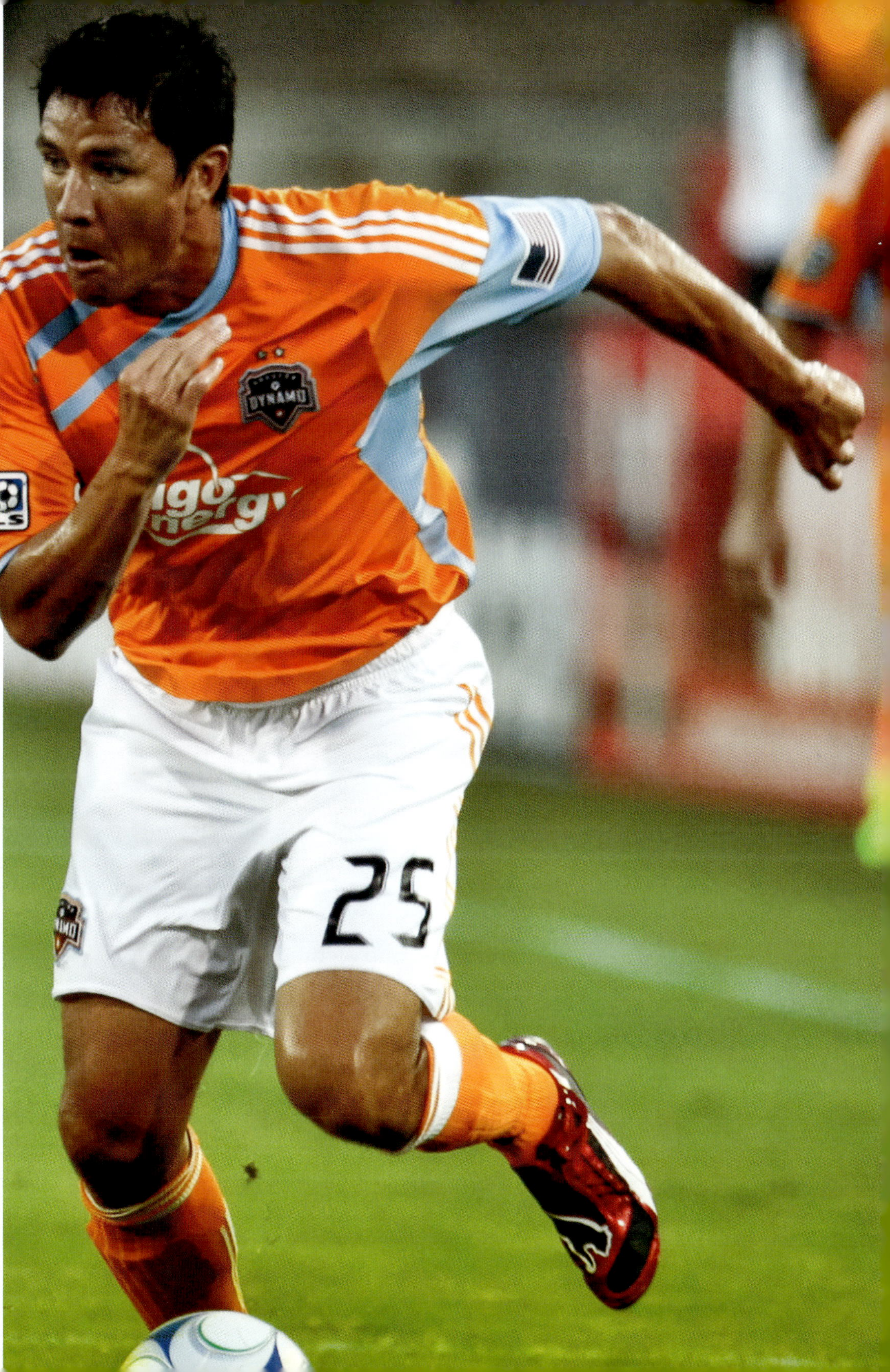
DYNAMO
MLS
25

He then moved into the front office of the local National Women's Soccer League (NWSL) team, the Houston Dash.

Brad Davis also followed the club from San Jose and found his home in Houston. In 10 seasons with the Dynamo, the midfielder became the club leader in games played with a total of 271. He was a supreme striker of the ball and was often the team's first choice to take a free kick or corner kick. He was named Dynamo MVP four times and was runner-up for league MVP in 2011.

No Dynamo player has had a goal-scoring season like Mauro Manotas. The Colombian fired home 25 goals in all competitions in 2018, setting a club record. Manotas quickly rose up the all-time scoring leaders since signing with the club in 2015. In just six seasons with the Dynamo, Manotas scored 51 MLS goals, second only to Ching in team history.

CHING'S TESTIMONIAL

In soccer, a testimonial is a special sendoff match for a player who is retiring, usually after a long time with a single club. Brian Ching received this honor in 2013. Ching played for the Orange Team along with other Dynamo players from 2006 and 2007. They played against a White Team featuring many of Ching's other Dynamo and US national team teammates. Orange won 6–4, with Ching scoring five goals.

Brad Davis was a star midfielder for a decade in Houston.

Defender Bobby Boswell and goalkeeper Pat Onstad team up to stop a shot in a 2009 playoff match against Seattle.

STEADY IN DEFENSE

For the Dynamo's first five seasons, Pat Onstad was Mr. Reliable in goal. Onstad was already an experienced pro. The Canadian national team standout was 38 by the time he moved to

Houston with the Dynamo. But he showed he had plenty left in his tank, leading the team to two MLS Cup championships. That included making the title-clinching save in a penalty kick shootout in 2006. He retired in 2010 as the Dynamo leader in shutouts, saves, and appearances for a keeper.

Defender Bobby Boswell came to Houston in a trade after the 2007 season. He quickly established a place on the Dynamo's back line. And he rarely left the field, ranking fourth all-time in club appearances despite only playing six seasons. Boswell was the team's Defender of the Year three times and served as an occasional captain.

DaMarcus Beasley's career took him all over the world. He started in MLS, then went to the Netherlands, England, Scotland, Germany, and Mexico. He saw even more of the world with the US men's national team, for which he made 126 appearances and became the only man to play in four World Cups.

MR. INTERNATIONAL

DaMarcus Beasley was one of the most accomplished American players overseas. In addition to his stints in MLS, he also played in the Netherlands, England, Scotland, Germany, and Mexico. While he was with PSV in the Netherlands in 2005, Beasley became the first American to play in the semifinals of Europe's premier club tournament, the Champions League.

29

Beasley signed with Houston in 2014. He became a steady presence in defense, earning the team's Defensive Player of the Year award twice. Beasley won it for the second time in 2018. He retired from pro soccer in 2019 at the age of 37.

MIGHTY MIDFIELDERS

Stu Holden didn't play in Houston orange for long. But it was the start of an impressive but brief career that took him to one of the best leagues in the world. After playing college soccer at Clemson, Holden began his professional career with Sunderland in England. However, injuries kept him on the sidelines, and he returned to the United States to sign with the Dynamo in 2006.

He soon became a fan favorite and played on two MLS Cup–winning teams. Holden returned to England, signing with Bolton of the Premier League in 2010. But injuries cut his career short at age 29. Holden went on to become a top soccer broadcaster in the United States.

Another Dynamo original, Ricardo Clark, roamed midfield for Houston in two different stints. His first term lasted until 2009, after which he gave European soccer a try. He returned in 2012 and stayed with the club through 2017. Clark's best year

DaMarcus Beasley was one of many US national team stars to play for the Dynamo.

25 FOR 25

At the end of MLS' 25th season in 2020, the league named its 25 best players of all time. Two of them played for the Dynamo. Forward Dwayne De Rosario scored 24 goals for the Dynamo from 2006 through 2008 and was the 2007 MLS Cup MVP. Fellow forward Chris Wondolowski has scored more goals than any MLS player, though only four came while with the Dynamo from 2006 to 2009.

came in 2015 when he started every game and scored eight goals. He was named team MVP.

The Dynamo made midfielder Will Bruin the 11th overall in the 2011 MLS draft, and he hit the ground running by leading all rookies in goals. Bruin set a club record the next year with 16 goals in all competitions. Four of those came in the playoffs, including both goals in a 2–1 win over the Chicago Fire. When Bruin was traded after the 2016 season he stood in second place behind Ching in career goals with 57.

Will Bruin splits the Toronto defense to score a goal in 2012.

CHAPTER 4

DYNAMITE
MOMENTS

Perhaps the greatest moment in Dynamo history was the one that ushered it into existence. That announcement was made on December 15, 2005. Then the next day, the mayor of Houston welcomed coach Dominic Kinnear and players Wade Barrett and Pat Onstad to the steps of city hall.

By April the team was a reality. And it made an explosive start. Brian Ching single-handedly gave the Dynamo a 4–1 lead in the team's first game. With time winding down and Houston up three goals, a win was assured. But Alejandro Moreno wanted his team's new fans to have something else to remember.

Houston goalkeeper Pat Onstad celebrates after stopping New England's final shootout attempt to win the 2006 MLS Cup.

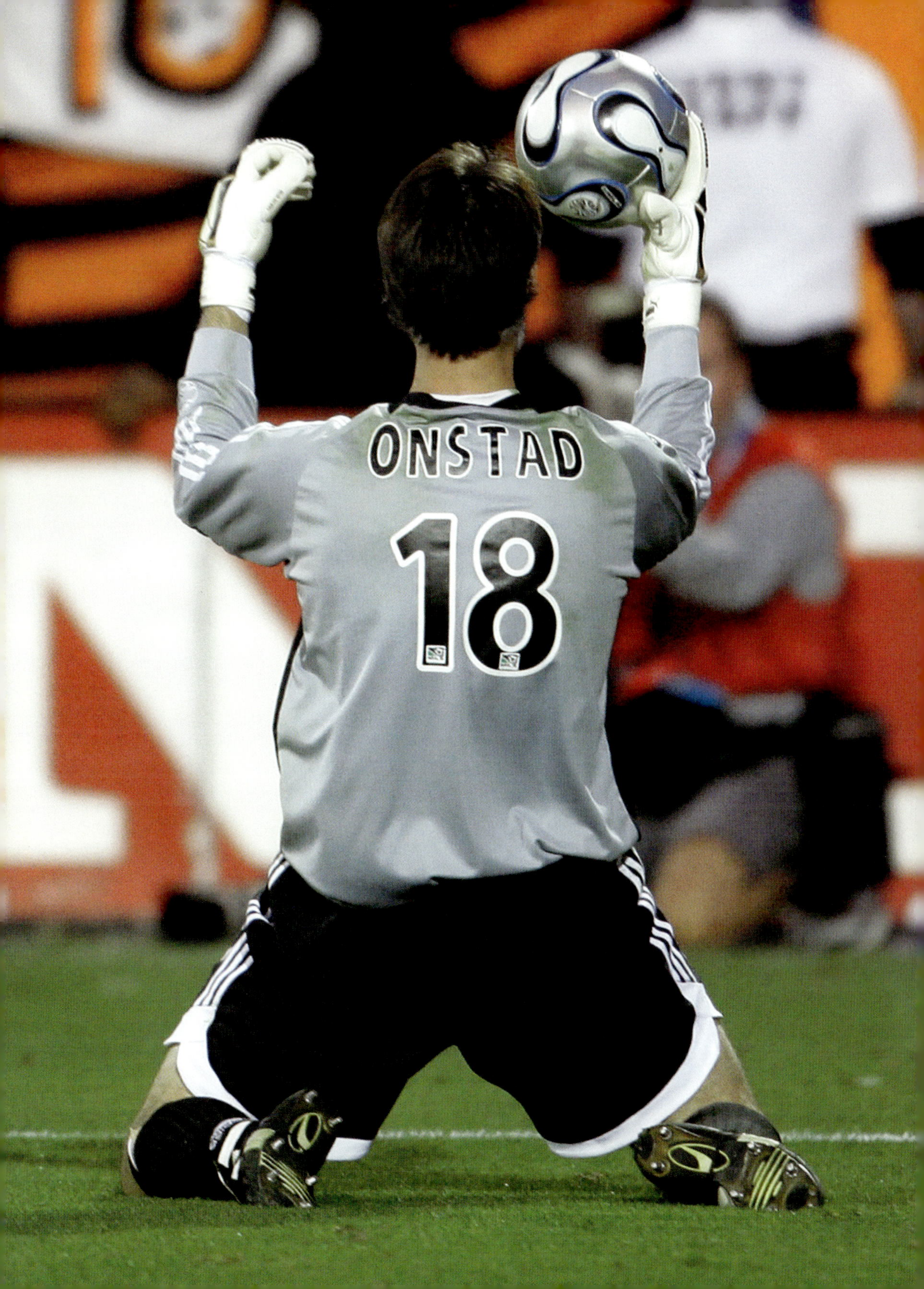
ONSTAD
18

The ball got chipped up into the air in the middle of the box. Moreno had his back to goal, but he never took his eyes off the ball. He jumped and fell backward, kicking straight up with his right foot. He met the ball perfectly, and it sailed into the back of the net. It was a rare bicycle kick that ended up being named the MLS Goal of the Week.

The rest of 2006 was a magical ride as the team won the MLS Cup in its first year in Houston. The Dynamo planned to take the city on another ride in 2007. Houston had a deep forward group with Ching leading the way. Chris Wondolowski, who went on to become the leading scorer in MLS history, was on that team but rarely cracked the starting lineup. The midfield was powered by Brad Davis and Stu Holden.

REPEATING AS CHAMPS

But at the end of May, the Dynamo had managed only two wins from eight matches. They had already lost five times. However, they would lose just three more from June through October, finishing with the third-best record in MLS. Houston had to go on the road to rival FC Dallas to open the playoffs. The Dynamo suffered a 1–0 loss and were faced with elimination. In the second game of the series, in Houston, the Dynamo again fell behind 1–0 at halftime.

Houston's Joseph Ngwenya reacts after scoring a huge goal against New England in the 2007 MLS Cup.

Second-half goals from Holden and Ching gave Houston a win in the match, but it only tied the total score of the series. So the match went to extra time. In the fifth minute, Ching scored again to put Houston on top. Three minutes later, Davis scored another just for good measure.

After shutting out Kansas City 2–0 in the conference final, Houston advanced to the MLS Cup. It was a rematch with the New England Revolution. And the previous year's nemesis, Taylor Twellman, put New England ahead in the 20th minute. That was the score at halftime.

In the 61st minute, Houston played the ball into the box. Forward Joseph Ngwenya received it and had an open shot. He failed to get a clean strike at first, but then recovered and fired a goal past the keeper.

Thirteen minutes later, Ngwenya received a long pass deep into Revolution territory. He used his dribbling skills to keep possession and pass out to a teammate, who sent in a crossing pass to the box where Dwayne De Rosario was waiting. De Rosario fired the ball off his head and into the back of the net for a 2–1 Dynamo lead.

New England had one prime chance to score in the 87th minute. Off a corner kick, the ball sailed perfectly into the

Dwayne De Rosario holds his trophy after being named MVP of the 2007 MLS Cup.

path of Jeff Larentowicz. His diving header rocketed toward Pat Onstad, but the Dynamo goalie made the save. Houston was able to run out the final few minutes to secure another

A replica cannon called *El Capitán* is the trophy that's on the line every time the Dynamo play FC Dallas.

championship victory. The Dynamo became the second team in MLS history to go back-to-back.

A HISTORIC DRAW

MLS teams haven't fared too well in the Concacaf Champions League, which features the best professional clubs from North and Central America and the Caribbean. These matches are especially exciting for Dynamo fans, many of whom also follow

Mexican league teams. The LA Galaxy won the 2000 tournament, but no MLS team repeated that feat in the next 20 years.

In 2008 Houston earned a historic point in Champions League competition. The Dynamo played Pumas UNAM in Mexico City. The match was a back-and-forth affair. Houston led 2–0. Then Pumas tied it. Then it was 3–2 Houston before Pumas took a 4–3 lead. Finally, Houston's Craig Waibel tied it at four. Houston became the first MLS team to earn a point on Mexican soil in the competition.

> ### TEXAS DERBY
> Houston's main rival is FC Dallas. The teams contest the Texas Derby every time they play. And at the end of the season, whichever team got the best of the other overall is awarded El Capitán. The trophy is a replica of an 18th-century cannon.

ANOTHER TROPHY AT LAST

For 10 seasons after the 2007 MLS Cup title, Houston went without a trophy. That changed in 2018. The team made its deepest run yet in the US Open Cup. And it was not an easy path to get there. Apart from a first-round win over an amateur team, Houston faced only MLS competition the rest of the way.

The semifinal against Los Angeles FC was a thriller. Houston took a 3–1 lead in the 75th minute, only to see LAFC strike back three minutes later. Then with time running out in the

A NEW HOME

The Dynamo have always played well at home. But when they opened BBVA Compass Stadium in 2012, they became even tougher to beat. Houston did not lose a match the first season in its new stadium. The Dynamo were unbeaten at home until a 1–0 loss to Sporting Kansas City on May 12, 2013. That ended a streak of 36 home matches without a loss, stretching back to 2011 at Robertson Stadium.

95th minute, LA's Diego Rossi scored his third goal of the game to send it to extra time. After 30 scoreless minutes, the match went to a penalty shootout. It took eight rounds, but Houston prevailed to advance to the final. Then the Dynamo shut out Philadelphia Union 3–0 to lift the US Open Cup for the first time.

The trophy came as a relief to longtime Dynamo fans. The team was a smash hit in its first few years in Houston. It was tough to duplicate that early run of success. But Dynamo fans were rewarded as their team started its climb back to the top.

Houston's Mauro Manotas celebrates the Dynamo's victory over Philadelphia in the 2018 US Open Cup final.

43

TIMELINE

2005	2006	2006	2007	2008
On December 15, MLS Commissioner Don Garber announces the San Jose Earthquakes will relocate to Houston for the 2006 season.	The renamed Houston Dynamo plays its first game on April 2. Brian Ching scores four goals in a 5–2 win over the Colorado Rapids.	On November 12, Houston wins the MLS Cup over the New England Revolution in a penalty kick shootout 4–3.	Houston repeats as MLS Cup champion, winning a rematch with the Revolution 2–1.	The Dynamo post the best record in the Western Conference for the first time but lose in the conference semifinals to the New York Red Bulls.

2012	2012	2013	2018	2020
Houston opens its new soccer-specific stadium, BBVA Compass Stadium.	Houston makes it to the MLS Cup final for the second year in a row, but both end in losses to the LA Galaxy.	The Dynamo's record 36-match home unbeaten streak comes to an end.	Houston beats Philadelphia Union 3–0 in the final of the US Open Cup to win that trophy for the first time.	The team officially changes its name to Houston Dynamo Football Club (FC) following the 2020 season.

TEAM FACTS

FIRST SEASON
2006

STADIUMS
Robertson Stadium (2006–11)
BBVA Stadium (2012–)

MLS CUP TITLES
2006, 2007

US OPEN CUP TITLES
2018

KEY PLAYERS
DaMarcus Beasley (2014–19)
Bobby Boswell (2008–13)
Will Bruin (2011–16)
Brian Ching (2006–13)
Ricardo Clark (2006–09, 2012–17)
Brad Davis (2006–15)
Dwayne De Rosario (2006–08)
Mauro Manotas (2015–20)
Pat Onstad (2006–10)

KEY COACHES
Dominic Kinnear (2006–14)
Tab Ramos (2020–)

MLS BEST XI SELECTIONS
Geoff Cameron (2009)
Ricardo Clark (2006)
Brad Davis (2011)
Dwayne De Rosario (2006, 2007)
Stu Holden (2009)
Eddie Robinson (2007)

MLS GOAL OF THE YEAR
Brian Ching (2006)

MLS SAVE OF THE YEAR
Pat Onstad (2009)

GLOSSARY

aggregate
The combined score of both games in a two-match series.

amateur
Someone who is not paid to perform an activity.

commissioner
The chief executive of a sports league.

conference
A subset of teams within a sports league.

corner kick
A free kick from a corner of the field near the opponent's goal.

draft
A system that allows teams to acquire new players coming into a league.

dribbling
The touches on the ball by a player as it is taken up the field.

extra time
Two 15-minute periods added to a game if the score is tied at the end of regulation.

folded
Went out of business.

free kick
An unguarded kick awarded to a team after an opponent's foul.

penalty kick shootout
A tiebreaking shootout after extra time to decide who wins a game.

rookies
First-year players.

strikers
Players whose primary responsibilities are to create scoring chances and score goals.

MORE INFORMATION

BOOKS

Kortemeier, Todd. *Total Soccer*. Minneapolis, MN: Abdo Publishing, 2017.

Marthaler, Jon. *Ultimate Soccer Road Trip*. Minneapolis, MN: Abdo Publishing, 2019.

Trusdell, Brian. *Soccer Record Breakers*. Minneapolis, MN: Abdo Publishing, 2016.

ONLINE RESOURCES

Booklinks
NONFICTION NETWORK
FREE! ONLINE NONFICTION RESOURCES

To learn more about the Houston Dynamo, please visit **abdobooklinks.com** or scan this QR code. These links are routinely monitored and updated to provide the most current information available.

INDEX

Barrett, Wade, 34
Beasley, DaMarcus, 29–30
Boswell, Bobby, 29
Bruin, Will, 21, 32

Ching, Brian, 7–12, 18–21, 24–26, 32, 34–38
Clark, Ricardo, 20–21, 30–32

Davis, Brad, 21, 26, 36–38
Dempsey, Clint, 8
De Rosario, Dwayne, 20–21, 32, 38

Franchino, Joe, 7

Harden, James, 22
Heaps, Jay, 8
Holden, Stu, 20–21, 30, 36–38

Kinnear, Dominic, 21, 34

Larentowicz, Jeff, 39

Manotas, Mauro, 22, 26
Marić, Marko, 22
Moreno, Alejandro, 34–36
Mullan, Brian, 10

Ngwenya, Joseph, 38

Onstad, Pat, 8–12, 28–29, 34, 39

Quintero, Darwin, 22

Ramos, Tab, 22
Reis, Matt, 10
Rossi, Diego, 42

Twellman, Taylor, 7–8, 38

Waibel, Craig, 41
Wondolowski, Chris, 32, 36

ABOUT THE AUTHOR

Anthony K. Hewson has followed American soccer since before the MLS days. Originally from San Diego, he now lives in the Bay Area with his wife and dogs.